I0471207

AudioBook Profits

How To Make Money by Turning Your Kindle, Paperback and Hardcover Book into Audio.

By Omar Johnson

Table of Contents

Chapter I: Introduction

You have completed an awesome e-book and you have uploaded it to Kindle and seen it show up on Amazon.com. It is very tempting now just to sit back and relax and think about all of the money you will be making from the awesome e-book sales to come. And yet don't you want to share your story with all of the possible ears in the world? Wouldn't it be wonderful to make even more money by making your book available in an audio format?

Yes indeed, this would in fact be awesome for you! It will allow you to gain an entirely new audience while creating an additional income stream. But wait a second.....you're not a big name publisher like Simon and Schuster, Random House or Harper Collins so how would you get your audiobook published and distributed to the masses? The answer and the solution lies with a company called ACX.

In 2011, Audible an Amazon subsidiary launched ACX which is short for Audiobook Creation Exchange. ACX essentially is a marketplace where professional authors, agents, publishers, and other Rights Holders can post fallow audiobook rights. ACX was started with the intentions of it being the prime supplier of audiobooks in the world for sites like Amazon, the ITunes store, and Audible.com. Audible which became a subsidiary of Amazon in 2008 has become a supreme giant in the marketplace and they have become in a short period of time the largest producer of audiobooks in the world.

They were the first supplier of audio content that had a membership program which enabled the listener to customize their experience by offering a variety of choices. And ACX brought the revolution home allowing for everyday authors to produce audiobooks of their own work, without a publisher.

In the past if an audiobook was going to be produced it would be done at the direction of a publisher with a producer in a very expensive studio. The issue with that is most authors would never have their work turned into audiobooks since it was just about impossible with all of the limitations of time and expense. To be able to produce a book in a home studio that was available for international distribution was revolutionary and almost deemed impossible.

However, ACX was able to quickly prove to authors as well as big traditional publishing houses that this was indeed possible and there was in fact a huge need for audiobooks. Of the 100,000 books which were published in a given year in 2009 less than 5,000 were audiobooks. As a result of ACX creating the ultimate exchange for authors, narrators, producers and publishers there has been a tremendous growth of audiobooks in the marketplace since that period of time. In fact, a whopping ten times as many titles were produced via ACX in 2012 as in 2011!

Since most consumers purchase around 17 audiobooks a year ACX realized the ability to tap into the market and to offer authors the chance to dominate it. This is a market which is virtually untapped at the moment and allows authors to make a huge impact on their readers. These days writing is not controlled by the publishers, the fate of the writer is determined by the writer. The ability to produce a quality audiobook is now at the fingertips of the author with a few home studio set up elements and a little Audacity.

E-books are wonderful, and hardcover and paperback books are great, but not everyone in the world has time to actually read a screen or to hold a hard copy book. Audible offers over 100,000 different audiobooks today to the market and they range in every kind of content from technology to erotica. The varied topics as well as the harried pace of life have increased the level of demand for audiobooks to an all-time level of popularity.

What better time is there than listening to your favorite book while you are working out, feeding the dog, or folding laundry? Mundane tasks which were before the drudgery of everyday life are now becoming times when a person can enjoy just a few minutes of their favorite author. The audiobook business in the U.S. is a 2 billion dollar a year industry. A few things have given a massive rise to audiobooks:

- IPods and IPads as well as computers have made audiobooks accessible anywhere.
- Audiobooks are being used for learning by universities and employers.
- Self Help books are also very popular in this way as they are being consumed constantly with the goal of making improvements to exercise, wellness, wealth and other topics.
- People simply have less time and want to enjoy a book by listening to it, for these reason audiobooks are the way to go.

Having an audiobook present on the market is a great way to make more money from a project which is already complete. In addition to having a project already on the market you can greatly connect with your readers and extend your book's reach. People who do not normally buy hardcover and paperback books buy audiobooks. There is no better way to make additional money, and to extend your reach to other readers than to narrate your own audiobook.

By listening to the writer using their own intonations and sounds the reader is much more easily able to get an idea of the characters and their characteristics. For this reason it is very fun and amazing for authors to share their own voice with fans. Once an author sets this precedent fans will be looking forward to hearing the author bring the stories to life through their own voice.

Do you remember when you were a little child and it was around Halloween or maybe you were camping on a stormy night. Do you remember sitting with friends and listening to them tell ghost stories around the campfire?

Part of what made that experience so memorable and endearing is the spooky environment. And another part of that experience is the entire part of hearing the sounds in their voice and the way that their pitch would be raised or lowered when describing the events of the story. What also kept you glued to your seat and connected to the story was how the story was being narrated with the proper tone, pitch, pace and intonation. Part of what we will discuss in this book is how to be a great story teller and how to share your thoughts and your ideas with the world through great and amazing narration.

Narrating your own audiobook gives readers a new way to plug into the experience and be a part of the creative process of the writer. When you are reading a biography for example of a famous person, do you not find yourself trying to imagine how that person would sound and what they would bring to the table if they were in fact sharing the story on their own? If you were able to interview the person who was telling the story and then trying to translate that experience through your own voice, this is what the audience wants to hear.

In the media of sound there is a unique connection that you do not get from holding a physical copy of a book. That is because the experience is actually translated through the sounds and intonations of another person and their ability as a story teller to immerse you in that experience. This is one reason that audiobooks are in fact so popular as well is that the sound of one person talking to another and sharing their experience is one that can hardly translate into electronic clicks or into pages.

In this book, I will show you all of the basics which include how to create a home studio, how to record, how to use the software and also how to be a successful story teller and narrator. And if you don't want to narrate your own book I will show you how to find, select and choose a narrator. In addition, you will also learn how to market your audiobook. And who knows you may have opened the door not only to narrating your own book, but maybe into sharing your gifts with others by becoming a voice over artist as well.

Grab some coffee, tea or whatever it is that you drink and grab a seat in a comfy chair and prepare for a new experience which will assist you in becoming the star narrator and audiobook author that you always knew you were.

Chapter II: Setting Up a Home Recording Studio

Building a home recording studio 30 years ago would have seemed unfathomable because of the high cost associated with such a task. During that time period if you wanted to record something you would have had to book time in a recording studio and pay big bucks. In fact, booking time in a professional recording studio was left to record companies and people that were associated with the recording industry.

However, as technology advanced and recording equipment was made readily available to the masses at reasonable and affordable prices building a home recording studio became an easily obtainable goal to people who have always wanted a DIY (do it yourself) alternative to recording. The home recording studio revolution to the delight of the independent artist was ushered in.

To set up an efficient and effective home recording studio that will enable you to record your audiobook is a simple and easy task. All you need is some space and an ample enough budget for the equipment that you will need and you will be able to produce a quality audiobook like a professional in no time. To assist you in this process, I'm going to show you exactly what you need to ensure your success. So without further delay here we go.

Equipment Needed:

Computer

Obviously you are going to need a computer in your home recording studio set up and if you don't have one you need to purchase one. It is one home studio recording essential that you can't bypass or skip over. There are a few things you need to consider in making sure that your computer is more than adequate enough to handle recording tasks.

1) **Processing speed and amount of memory.** Your computer needs to have the processing speed and memory to handle the recording tasks at hand in addition to also being able to handle the other programs and resources that you presently have running on your computer. To accomplish this, your computer needs to have a lot of RAM or memory and a quality processor.

    In regards to memory, I suggest that you have no less than 4 Gigabytes of RAM. Most recording, editing and mixing software have minimum system requirements in terms of speed, memory and storage availability and you have to make sure that your computer meets those minimum specifications of the software that you choose.

2) **Hard Drive.** You are going to be using a great amount of storage space because audio files are pretty large. For example, when I narrated and recorded the first two chapters of my audiobook "The Fine Art of Writing the Next Best Seller on Kindle" the audio files that I created for each chapter combined to take up at least 1 Gigabyte of storage on my computer.

So if you are purchasing a new computer specifically to handle all of your recording, editing and mixing tasks make sure that you purchase one that has a large hard drive with a large amount of storage space. 1 Terabyte of storage capability should be more than enough.

Also make sure that you purchase a fast hard drive. A fast hard drive will reduce the chances of unwanted pops and clicks during recording and playback and somewhat speed up your computer's processes. I highly recommend that you purchase at least a 7200 rpm hard drive with a 32mb cache.

If the computer that you are considering for purchase or if the computer that you presently have hard drive isn't large enough you can always purchase an external hard drive and connect it to your computer via USB expanding your storage capabilities.

3) **Sound Card.** If you have a basic sound card installed on your computer you should strongly consider upgrading it to one with more capabilities because factory installed sound cards that come with computers are not usually robust enough to produce high quality recordings.

Microphone

The microphone that you choose depends entirely on the equipment that you will be using. Now of course regardless of the type of equipment that you will be using, you can't use the basic microphone headset that you use with your computer or any other low quality microphone for that matter, because you will produce a poor sounding audiobook that lacks quality and one that will be rejected by the audiobook distributors when they put your audiobook through the quality control process.

Personally, I have two different recording set ups in my house (of course you only need one) that require two different types of microphones. I have a recording room where I use a Pro Tools set up. Now if you don't mine investing some money in a super quality recording, editing and mixing software, then Pro Tools is the way to go as it is the standard in the recording industry.

Anyway in this particular Pro Tools set up, I use an audio interface called an Mbox which is basically an external device that allows you to plug in a microphone into a separate input and you also are able to plug a pair of headphones into another separate input. The audio interface connects to your computer and allows you to monitor and hear what you record while you are recording it and it allows you to also listen to what you have recorded during playback.

The microphone that I use for this particular set up is a Shure KSM32 condenser microphone. A condenser microphone allows you to produce high quality vocal recordings and I highly suggest that you use a condenser microphone regardless of your recording set up. However, it is imperative that you choose the right type of condenser microphone that matches your recording set up.

For instance, the Shure KSM32 condenser microphone that I use for my Pro Tools set up uses an XLR cable that attaches directly to the microphone and the opposite end of that XLR cable connects directly to the audio interface box.

I use a much different condenser microphone in my second recording set up where I use a free recording, editing and mixing software called Audacity. This particular set up does not have an external audio interface box like the one I use for Pro Tools. In fact, it has an audio interface and mixer built directly into the microphone. The name of this microphone is a Samson

G Track microphone. It is a USB enabled condenser microphone which allows you to connect it directly to your computer via a USB cable.

Another great thing about the Samson G Track microphone is that it has headphone management built into it which basically means that you plug your headphones directly into the microphone not the computer.

The Samson G Track essentially performs three jobs:

1) It converts your voice or performance to digital and sends it down the USB cable for recording.
2) It converts the USB digital show from the computer back to analog.

3) It has an internal headphone mixer. The G-Track can mix your existing track playback and your new, live performance so you can listen to both.

If you plan on recording straight into your computer without the use of an external audio interface like the Mbox you will need to purchase a USB enabled condenser microphone that has an audio interface built into the microphone. I highly recommend that you use the Samson G Track microphone if you are planning on using Audacity. You can purchase one new on Ebay for around $80-$100 or you can buy it for around $120 online at SamAsh.com.

Another alternative to the Samson G Track microphone is the Blue Microphones Yeti Pro USB & XLR Multi-Pattern Condenser Microphone. It is much pricier at $250 but it has superior quality. You can also purchase the Blue Microphones Yeti Pro USB & XLR Multi-Pattern Condenser Microphone online at SamAsh.com.

If you plan on using an external audio interface like the Mbox here is a list of some really quality condenser microphones that you can use: The price ranges vary, but I'm sure you can find a condenser microphone to fit your budget.

RODE NTK Cardioid Tube Condenser Microphone

The RODE NTK is basically a quality tube microphone that is designed for recording professionals who want what only the best can offer. It delivers a wide dynamic range and ultra low noise when recording. The price of the RODE NTK Cardioid Tube Condenser Microphone is $530. This may seem steep to some, but if you are looking for a quality microphone to invest in then you should strongly consider the RODE NTK as an option.

Shure SM27-SC Large Diaphragm Side Address Condenser Microphone

The SM27 is a large diaphragm cardioid microphone with low self-noise that picks up vocal nuances with clarity. Condenser microphones are usually large diaphragm or small diaphragm. A large diaphragm microphone in my opinion is usually the best choice for recording vocals because you get a more deep sound. The Shure SM27-SC is a nice quality large diaphragm microphone and it is priced at $300

AKG Perception 420 Condenser Microphone

The AKG Perception 420 is a multi pattern large diaphragm condenser microphone that has three selectable polar patterns: cardioids, omni directional or figure eight. This allows a wide range of stereo making techniques and the ability to make incredible ambient recordings. It is priced at $249.

Shure PG27-LC

The Shure PG27-LC is a large diaphragm cardioid condenser microphone that provides a natural and clear reproduction of vocals. It is priced at $149. I know that I've been mentioning in our discussion of microphones cardioid microphones and you are probably wondering what exactly is a cardioid microphone so let me explain.

A cardioid microphone is named based on its pattern of sensitivity. A cardioid polar pattern picks up most of the sound from in front of the microphone while minimal noise is picked up from the rear and marginal noise is picked up from the sides which makes it less susceptible to feedback in high volume settings.

Condenser Microphones for Under $100

$200- $500 for a condenser microphone maybe out of your budget range so here are a couple of condenser microphones that are priced at under $100 and also remember that you don't necessarily have to buy a new condenser microphone you can save yourself a great deal of money by purchasing a used one on Ebay.

AKG Perception 120 Condenser Microphone

The AKG Perception 120 is a cardioid low mass diaphragm condenser microphone that delivers a clear sound with accurate sonic detail and it is reasonably priced at $99.

Samson C01 Condenser Microphone

The Samson C01 is a large diaphragm condenser microphone that is great for recording vocals. It has a large 19mm diaphragm that produces a smooth flat frequency response and it is reasonably priced at $79.99

MXL 770 Condenser Microphone

The MXL 770 is a cardioid condenser microphone that delivers a silky up front high end and a solid low frequency sound. It is reasonably priced at $99.

Microphone Stand

You will definitely need a microphone stand in your home recording studio to keep your microphone in place while you are recording. A microphone stand is also used to position the microphone exactly as you want it. For all of the newbies out there you can't hold a microphone in your hand while you are recording. It's an absolute no-no. Your microphone must be mounted when you record.

Microphone stands vary in price and I suggest that you don't break the bank to purchase one. However, what I highly recommend is that you purchase a sturdy and durable one.

Shock Mount

A shock mount is basically a device that is used to isolate a microphone from vibration. The elastic on a shock mount is used to separate the microphone from the microphone stand which eliminates noise caused by vibration from the floor.

Shock mounts are usually included with the purchase of a microphone, but if you have to buy one they are relatively inexpensive.

Pop Filter

A pop filter is a small round piece of acoustically transparent mesh that sits between your mouth and the microphone and its job is to eliminate plosives and sibilance that occur when recording words that have "P", "S" and "Sh" sounds. These particular letters and sounds tend to "pop" the microphone with a sudden burst of air in the case of plosives ("P" sounds) and in the case of "S" and "Sh" sounds cause a high pitch hissing noise which is referred to as sibilance.

Plosives will destroy your recording by clipping and distorting the signal to the microphone as well as to the input channel that you are using to record your vocals on. By using a pop filter you will avoid having these types of problems. A good pop filter will cost anywhere between 15 – 25 dollars.

Headphones and Studio Monitors

You need a great pair of quality headphones and studio monitors which are sometimes referred to as reference speakers in your home recording studio. Headphones allow you to monitor what you are recording and they also allow you to hear every nuance of your recording in playback.

It is not necessary to spend an arm and a leg for a pair of quality headphones and you have to be careful not to be duped by some salesperson who will attempt to try to get you to spend $300-$400 for a pair of headphones so that they can earn a commission. I had my share of pricy headphones and none of them have yet to beat my pair of Sony MDR ZX 100 stereo headphones that I paid $20 for.

Studio monitors are different from regular speakers because they are designed to deliver a perfectly flat frequency response. What this basically means is that you are hearing your recording exactly as it is digitally without any frequency adjustment.

When choosing studio monitors for your home recording studio make sure that you purchase "near field" models, because these types of monitors are designed to be listened to from 1 yard away with the purpose of eliminating any effects due to the acoustics of your room.

Audio Interface

What exactly is an audio interface? An audio interface is a nifty device that you connect to your computer that allows the computer to send and receive audio data to and from the outside world. The audio interface contains an analogue to digital converter which allows it to convert the analogue sound coming from your microphone to a digital format so that your computer can read it.

An audio interface also serves the purpose of upgrading the sound output of your computer. This is important because the factory installed sound card that came with your computer is not robust enough to produce high quality recordings. Your computer also doesn't have many input and output ports, but a good audio interface does which allows you to connect other devices to it.

If you purchase a condenser microphone like the Samson G Track or the Blue Microphones Yeti Pro which have audio interfaces built directly into them, it is not necessary to purchase an external audio interface. There are many external audio interfaces on the market and their prices vary, but the one that I highly recommend is the Mbox by Avid. It costs about $500 and they include the Pro Tools software for free. You can visit Avid at the following website address:

http://www.avid.com

Recording Software

Recording software allows you to record, edit, mix and master your audiobook with ease right on your computer. There are many paid and free options available in the marketplace and on the internet. Some of the paid options for recording software include Cubase, Cakewalk, Ableton, Motu and my favorite Pro Tools.

Some of the free options include Anvil Studio, Kristal Audio Engine, Quartz AudioMaster and my personal favorite Audacity which I highly recommend because of its simplicity and ease of use. Audacity works on Windows (Windows 2000/XP/Vista/Windows 7/Windows 8), The Mac (Mac OS X 10.4 or later) and GNU/Linux. You can download Audacity for free at the following website address:

http://www.audacity.sourceforge.net

Later on I am going to give you a complete tutorial on how to record your audiobook in Audacity.

Conversely, the paid options have extensive digital interfaces that mimic the studio gear that you see in those high powered recording studios. They also allow you to create an even better sound by allowing you to use plug-ins. For example, Pro Tools comes with over 75 virtual instruments, effects, sound processing, and utility plug-ins, some of which emulate the sounds of classic hardware processors, amps, and instruments.

Comfortable Chair

Some narrators prefer narrating a book from the comforts of a chair and others prefer narrating standing up. Regardless of your personal preference, you still need a comfortable chair for your home recording studio, because you'll be definitely using it to listen to many hours of playback, editing, mixing etc. and you want to be as comfortable as possible.

If you plan on sitting down in a chair while you narrate your book, you must make certain that your chair doesn't "squeak" or make little noises as you move around a little while you are recording, because if it does you will be spending extra time editing these little noises out.

Chapter III: Sound Proofing Acoustic Treatment and Creating a Quality Recording Environment

Now that you know the equipment that you will need to produce an audiobook, you have to ensure that you choose the ideal recording space in your home. In addition, once you decide on the actual recording space you have to give strong consideration to sound proofing and sound control. So the question begs where are you going to set up your home recording studio?

The answer to that question is you should set up your home recording studio in the quietest place in the house. The quietest place in your house should be free of both outside noise and inside noise. Outside noise would be things like birds chirping, dogs barking in your yard or your neighbor's yard that can seep through and enter your recording space and be picked up by the microphone when you are recording.

Outside noise also include things like rustling leaves, wind blowing, airplanes flying overhead, car horns, children noisily playing outside, ambulance and police sirens etc. These outside noises can ruin your recording and are very difficult to edit out, because they occur randomly throughout a recording. If you have a pair of quality headphones you will actually hear these outside noises become part of your recording while you are recording no matter how faint the sound is.

Speaking from personal experience this can be a big pain in the butt as it interferes with your rhythm and momentum while you are narrating. You could be really in the flow narrating your book then all of a sudden you hear birds chirping or rain pouncing against your air conditioner causing you to abruptly stop and end your recording. To further add to the frustration you have to spend extra time editing out the noise that you've recorded to salvage your recording.

Inside noise would be the sound of your telephone or cell phone ringing, the humming sound coming from the refrigerator, the T.V. playing in the other room, the sound of an air conditioner etc. These natural sounds have always been around us however, we only seriously notice them when we begin to record. I guess that's just how the brain is wired in that we pay strict attention to the things that we focus on.

Once you have selected the quiet room that you are going to use for your recording space you must prepare it. The first thing that you should do is make sure that all of the windows are tightly shut, because if air can get through then so can sound. Also check for drafts because if there is a draft it has the ability to rattle a window and create unwanted noise.

The sound of the draft can actually make its way onto your recording. So if you have drafty windows make sure that you weather strip them with foam weather stripping. This will alleviate the problem. You must also make sure that all doors are shut closed, because if they are not the natural circulating air will cause them to open a little which naturally creates a creaking sounding noise.

If you live in an apartment and your recording room contains a steam radiator for heat, make sure the steam valve is shut off before you record, because if it is not it will emit a whistling type of noise that has the equivalent sound of a boiling whistling teapot. Turn off all air conditioners regardless if they are the ones that stick outside of your window or central air because you don't want to pick up any humming noises in your recording. Also check for ticking clocks, a squeaking chair, ceiling fans and anything thing else that can potentially make noise.

There is also the natural noise that comes from your computer that you obviously can't get rid of, but you can definitely isolate it. You can isolate it in several different ways. If you are using a tower computer you should consider placing it under your desk or as far away from the microphone as possible. This eliminates the possibility of the microphone picking up the noise from the computer fan.

If that approach doesn't do the trick then you should set up sound baffles around your computer which aids in blocking the sound and eliminating the noise. You can create your own sound baffles by purchasing acoustic foam from your local recording store or online at SamAsh.com or Auralex.com. You also have to purchase foam core panels so that you can attach the acoustic foam to them with some spray adhesive. This gives you instant sound baffles.

When you have finished sound proofing your recording space and eliminated all potential noise generating objects and scenarios, it is now time to perform a test. The way that you would perform a test is by recording silence. You do this by turning your microphone gain or volume all the way down and pressing record.

Once you have recorded the silence listen to it in playback. Do you hear any noise? Strange sounds? If no then great! However, if you in fact hear any peculiar sounds or noise try to locate their origin and eliminate them. Listen intently do you hear any electrical noise? Any hiss or humming? If so then this could be the result of bad grounding, your cables being entangled or your audio cables can be too close to your power cord or computer monitor.

You must fix this before proceeding any further, because if you narrate your audiobook under these conditions you will produce a poor quality recording that is full of hum and hiss.

Acoustic Treatment

After going through the process of sound proofing your recording room it's now time to acoustically treat it. The concept of acoustic treatment is this. Everything in your home recording studio essentially revolves around sound waves and those sound waves are consistently and continuously bouncing all around your recording room producing reflections. The big bucks professional recording studios are specifically built from the ground up to handle these reflections. Your home recording studio is not afforded this luxury so it must be acoustically treated to bring it up to par.

Your recording room whether you have it in a house or an apartment more than likely is rectangular in shape because it is probably located in a bedroom or a home office which isn't conducive to recording and mixing. For example, if you clap your hands while standing in your recording room you will probably hear a slight echo.

Most rooms have an echo and to hammer home my point have you ever been in a room that had no furniture? When you talked in that particular room or when someone spoke to you didn't you hear a bright echo? Well you don't want this echo in your recording because you can't remove it. What you actually want recorded is just your voice and no echo. This is referred to as a dry recording.

To further explain how sound works when it travels let's look at the example of sound hitting your walls in your recording room. When this happens the sound either reflects, is absorbed or is transmitted through the actual medium. In the case of a wall it usually reflects high frequencies that produce echoes.

Of course you want to keep these echoes under control and the best way to accomplish this is by acoustically treating your recording room to absorb sound. There are many things that will absorb sound and here are a few of them.

1) Carpeted floors
2) Rugs
3) Absorption panels
4) Bass traps
5) Foam
6) Blankets
7) Heavy Drapes or Curtains

The bottom line is, in order for you to produce a high quality audiobook it is essential that you create a high quality recording environment. This entails having a proper acoustically treated recording space, the proper recording equipment and effectively sound proofing your home recording studio to keep out all extraneous sounds and noises.

If you need further assistance in regards to this, I suggest that you contact a company called Auralex

located at the following web address
http://www.auralex.com and they will give you a free
recording room analysis. They'll analyze your recording
space and will offer you a viable solution.

Chapter IV: Narrating Your Own Book

Well you have taken on the task of self-narrating
your book, but now you are tasked with wearing the
many hats of many different characters and performing
their roles can be slightly difficult. How do you jump
from one person to another at a moment's notice in the
blink of an eye and plan this so that the execution is
flawless?

Unless you have a professional acting career or
have performed on stage before this can seem very
difficult. The main difference though is even if you have
performed on stage you still were only one character.
You were not responsible for the entire success or failure
of an audiobook based on your performance.

Readers will put down an audiobook based on the
quality of the narration. If they find the narrator to be
annoying, whiny or not someone that they can identify
with the book is sunk. I am going to give you some
common sense tips and tricks on how to approach this
slightly complicated and fun task.

Before you can really understand how to portray a person you must think about who they are and what makes them tick. Knowing your characters will be critical to understanding them and giving an effective portrayal. As the author you already know more than anyone else about the characters, but sometimes when you are writing maybe you didn't develop them to the level that you could have.

For example, did you really think about what kind of home life the mechanic who was working on the car in your book had? As you are portraying his voice you will have to think about all of these minute details. What kind of accent did he speak with? How would he express his words in different situations?

1. **Imagine a day in the life of your characters!** What do they have for breakfast? How do they eat their toast? When they are drinking their coffee do they slurp it? All of these things are very important to think about for your major characters. Think about their mannerisms and all of the different things they do to incorporate it into your performance for believability.

   So if you are like me and have never acted sometimes it can seem a bit outlandish to imagine yourself portraying all the different characters and their mannerisms. Practice makes perfect as the old saying goes. So how do you practice your voices and characters?

2. **Take it to the mirror.** Try standing in front of the mirror and practicing your new characters personalities. Try to more than talk like them; try to walk like them and to think like them. Get deep and in the recesses of their mind and think about how they do everything. Once you get in this kind of a zone, practice some more and try in earnest to channel your character. Then try transitioning between the different characters from one moment to the next in the mirror so that you will be able to be fluid when you narrate and record.

Transitioning from one personality to the next can be very challenging when you are performing. Think of a few different key elements that can be trigger thoughts for you on a certain person or personality.

3. **Trigger Thoughts.** An easy way to think of a trigger thought for a character is to imagine what you think of when someone

mentions your favorite celebrity. For example, when people mention Jennifer Lopez what do you imagine? When someone says Garfield you probably think of lasagna. Think of these different words with the characters and you will be able to jump back and forth easily from one character to the next.

How do you keep all of the characters and all of the details straight? Now that you have so many different things and people to remember how are you going to do it? I know I have sticky notes all over my refrigerator, and my laptop sometimes with things that I need to do and I still have issues with all the facts.

4. **Diagram it out!** Have you ever had it happen to you, you know all the facts and then the second that you are ready to deliver a speech you forget everything? Well I am very certain that this can happen in the recording booth as well. To avoid this make yourself a few quick cheat sheets that will help you remember the little nuances of your characters and the elements of the story.

For example, jot down things like "sound irritated when narrating this part of the story because this is when the main character John is upset and pissed off with everyone". This will help you remember if you get in the position where you can't or are nervous and have issues grabbing the facts.

Maybe you also have an added layer of complication with an accent to learn for a character you are narrating. If you are like me you don't wander around and pick up on different kinds of accents so for this reason pulling one out of your back pocket may not be a possibility. But if you have to learn how to do an accent how do you do it?

5. **Get your British on or fill in the blank.** So if you have a character that is Spanish, or French, or Chinese and you are not you already have a difficult task on your hands of understanding how to properly pronounce, annunciate and copy the accent. Where do you even begin?

   a. Realize there are two kinds of languages pitch and syllabic. What does that mean? For a non-linguist here is the 2 cent definition. A syllabic language is one that focuses on the accent of the words and stresses the pronunciation of consonants.

A pitch language focuses on the sounds of the vowels and not of their hard pronunciation but on their intricacy. If you have never spoken an Asian language before it becomes very difficult for a western speaker to mimic it without practice. Get a few scripts or words in the language of the accent you are practicing and read the lines.

b. If you can run those practice lines by a native speaker of the language and see what they think of your pronunciation. If you cannot find a native speaker check online for free language learning forums. There you can meet and communicate with speakers who are trying to learn English and they will help you for free.

c. If you can master the pronunciation of words in the native tongue you will

easily master the words in English
with the accent at that point.

d. Practice, practice and practice again.
Say the words in the native language
and then in English to assist in getting
yourself into the mindset of being that
character and delivering the
performance. Remember that if you
have a down day that you will lose
some of what you have worked so hard
to gain. Make sure you are practicing
these different accents for at least 15
minutes a day.

Now that you are practicing the
accents and the mannerisms of the
characters the next step is to practice
the script of the audiobook itself in
front of the mirror. This way you can
see how the performance will go and
also how it will change when you add
in multiple characters.

6. **Print it out and check it out in the
mirror.** Print a copy of the script, a hard
copy so you do not have to go back and
forth between the computer screen and
anything else. This will eliminate

distractions from you while you are working on your delivery of your material. Here are some keys to a good practice session:

a. Turn off your cell phone. It is hard to concentrate on what you are doing with a phone ringing in the background.

b. Kick out all pets, children, spouses and roommates so that you can practice and be as silly as necessary and be focused on the task at hand.

c. Go to a quiet and private place, if your practice room is grand central station or you can't find a place to go. Think of a place you would go if you were going to perform a meditation or something else you needed to be very focused for. Then grab your mirror and go to that location.

d. Plan on swapping back and forth between all of the different characters so you can get used to the flow from one personality to the next.

Now you are almost ready to know all of your characters as though they were close friends and to portray them via audiobook for the world to see and yet there is still one more wildcard factor here. And that wildcard is the recording itself.

7. **Record Your Practice and Delivery!**
More than just making a lovely recording of your voice for posterity you need to listen to your delivery and see how you are doing flowing from one character to the next. Are you for example running your words together in one point of the script while the rest is eloquently expressed with no issues? These are the little things that you need to notice now while you are practicing so you can determine how to fix them.

Aside from just recording yourself when you are making these jumps you need to be listening to yourself with headphones so you can hear the minute details. Without headphones it is impossible to hear the specific traits of your voice.

Are you starting to have bad dreams about your characters? When you close your eyes do you imagine them lurking around the corner? Are you having dreams about your teeth falling out? All of these dreams and thoughts are indicators that you may in fact be over practicing.

8. **Know when to stop!** If you have done everything you can in one day and are feeling burned out know when to take a break. Maybe you just aren't delivering well, or you feel there is nothing else that can be gained by another round. If this is the case you need to know when to stop. If you ignore these signs and continue anyway your recording and delivery will suffer and the audience will know. Fatigue can wear on the voice just as much as it can on the mind. There is nothing to be gained by beating a dead horse other than a frustrated and tired you.

Well you should have all of the tools you need to portray any characters you like for your work now. But what if you are just still feeling anxious about the whole process? What can you do to relax and slow things down for a few moments?

How to Take a Breather

1. Turn everything off for 15 minutes, phones, computers, and electrical equipment, anything that can interrupt you.

2. Get relaxing music and turn it on for 15 minutes. Everyone should have at least 15 minutes in the course of the day for meditation. There is a reason that by law you are required to take a 15 minute break after 4 hours of work at a job. The main reason is burnout. If you do not take a break and keep on working the quality of the work will suffer and you will feel drained.

3. Sit in a quiet place. Find a cozy couch, a nice bean bag chair or somewhere you can relax while still sitting up as you don't want to fall asleep.

4. Close your eyes focus on imagining you are in a lovely and relaxing place.

5. Remember that you are the master of your performance and your audiobook, take the nervousness in your system and turn it into motivation to succeed and give a great performance.

Hopefully now you have a better idea of how to take an amazing book and perform an awesome narration. And yet remember that in order to do that you must be able to also give great characterizations to the characters you bring life too. All of the littlest details are in fact the items which will bring your audience back for more and assist them in their craving to be transported through your story by your voice.

Chapter V: How To Narrate A Perfect Beginning, Middle And Ending

Often times there are a lot of questions related to how to narrate an audiobook. What sometimes happens in narration is that the narrator starts off strong, and gets lost somewhere in the middle sometimes losing the passion and the verve that was delivered in the beginning of the manuscript. There will be a very strong finish generally, but sometimes the listener gets a bit lost and never makes it to the end because of the issues with the delivery in the middle.

It is important to remember that when you are delivering narration in an audiobook it is an interactive experience and ultimately that means that it must be handled in the right way. What does this mean to the narrator explicitly? It means there should be no lull in the middle of the manuscript.

Everything needs to be upbeat and continual with no lulls. It is that one lull that will cause the listener to put down the book and not want to pick it up again. So, we are going to discuss how to narrate the beginning, the middle, and the end of an audiobook.

When narrating the beginning of an audiobook you are naturally full of passion and full of zeal. The research you were doing on the characters is fresh in your mind and you have been practicing in front of the mirror every day but taking all of the information you have been given, how do you begin strong?

Tips and Tricks for Narrating the Beginning of a Book

- Be comfortable in your environment. Find out where everything you need will be. For example: water, the restrooms, and that chair you need to sit in when you are exhausted and need a break.

- Warm up for at least 15 minutes and do your different character voices before getting behind the microphone.

- Make certain that when you are speaking that you are relaxing and taking your time.

- Do not rush through the recording because you are nervous, imagine as though you are talking to a friend about a topic and entertaining them with different voices and mimes.

- Make certain that you are listening to the playback and are not afraid to say that a do over might be necessary sometimes.

- Know what you are doing well and what you are not doing well so it can be corrected and you can improve upon the performance.

- Stay focused on every line and paragraph of the script; make sure you have that hard copy in your hand.

- Do not be afraid to write on the script and make notes of any areas which you think are important or noteworthy for yourself.

- Make certain that you get all of your bearings and feel comfortable so you can move on with the rest of the project. If there is an issue isolate it up front while recording so you are able to move onto other parts.

Tips and Tricks for an Amazing Narration of the Middle of the Audiobook

Now that you are off to the races and have made it to the middle part of the book you must make sure that you do not fall into the same pattern that many narrators fine themselves in, which is losing themselves and the interest of the reader in the middle of the manuscript. Remember that you must keep your focus or how can you expect the reader to?

- Stay active throughout the narration, stand and deliver so that you do not experience the blahs and translate that to the audience because you are bored sitting.

- Breathe deeply from your diaphragm so that you are keeping fresh life giving oxygen flowing throughout the delivery as this kind of deep breathing will produce a sense of stasis and well-being for you as you perform and will assist with any nervousness.

- If you find yourself having a difficult time with delivering the performance of a character stop the recording and focus instead on practicing the voice cadence and thoughts of that character. Transport yourself again in front of the mirror in your mind and regain channeling that character. If you are still having issues take a moment and step into the restroom and do a brief rehearsal in front of the mirror.

- Make certain that if you are feeling fatigued that you stop the recording and take a break. Although sometimes there is an overwhelming drive to hurry up and finish what is more important is knowing when quality is not being produced. Quality is what the listener will recognize and will most certainly stop listening to the book if the reading and narration is not interactive and engaging throughout the entire series.

- Remember some of the most engaging audiobooks can be some of the longest, for example the classic Ayn Rand's *Atlas Shrugged*. The book was so engaging even at 1125 pages because of the narration of the voice artists. As you are sitting there you are hanging on every word wanting more and when the CD or the tape ended you would stare at the stereo and think why? I want to know what happens. This is the formula for the success of a good audiobook.

- There should never be a dull moment and the listener shouldn't be staring at their iPod, iPhone, or other device thinking this part sucks! What's next?

Narrating the End of an Amazing Audiobook

As a narrator delivering an effective end to a book, especially one you wrote yourself could not be more important. What you are ensuring is that the listener will be left hungering for more whether looking for all of the material you have written or narrated or looking for perhaps the conclusion or the sequel.

The success of books like 50 Shades of Grey and the Twilight series all come from the fact that in the delivery of their art the authors left the audience feeling breathless. And the audience through the delivery of the audiobook felt so transported to that location that they in fact could not get enough and were clamoring for more.

- Remember the success of the end delivery of your book could make or seal the deal on other works you want to do as an author in the future. If you want to make a name for yourself closing out the book with the strongest performance you are able to give will be pivotal.

- If you are feeling fatigue or are getting tired remember that you must take breaks.

- Make certain to drink hot tea to keep the vocal cords limber and ready to perform at a moment's notice.

- Practice and practice again before going into the end portion of the book with all of the passion and fire that you as an author and artist are capable of giving.

- Make certain to read slowly and to focus again on all of the intricacies of the script and look at it line by line and word by word. Each paragraph is a brick in the wall of an amazing piece of art. So each one must be treated with the greatest attention and care.

Knowing the Difference in the Nuances of Narrating Fiction and Nonfiction

Now we have looked at narrating the different parts of the book and yet what about if you are narrating a fiction book or a non-fiction book? What are the differences between these two kinds of genres of writing? Fiction is just writing that completely comes from the ideas and mind of the author and is able to be created in any manner that the author chooses. While there are really two kinds of nonfiction, there is journalistic nonfiction which is based on research and facts on a subject. And there is biographical nonfiction, which is based on someone's actual life.

Both types of nonfiction have detailed intricacies that have to be taken into account in narration. For example in the case of the narration of biographical nonfiction to present a true picture of the main person or people involved in the story you have to research the mannerisms, figure of speech, the dialect and the overall expression of each and every character to be able to deliver a true representation and the realism of that time period to your listeners.

A vivid example of this is when I listened to Daniel Day Lewis portrayal of Lincoln in the hit movie Lincoln. It really transported me to that time period because the acting was so great he spoke like Lincoln, he walked like Lincoln, he had the mannerism of Lincoln and of course through the magic of makeup and Hollywood he even looked like Lincoln that I really felt that he was in fact Lincoln even though he was just playing the part. I guess others felt the same way and that's why he won an Oscar for being the best actor.

Narrating Fiction

Fiction is beautiful and inspiring in the aspect that it is completely the creation of the author which makes it the perfect asset for narration. It is the perfect asset for narration because as the author you know exactly how you developed the plot and the meaning of every scenario in that plot because it came from your mind. This will enable you to express the plot vividly in narration. You are also able to bring to life the setting and location of your story whether it is historical or a complete fantasy because you conjured it up.

However, narrating fictional characters can sometimes be a challenge to know how to develop voices for some of the characters that might not have any reference to people or to other characters in the literary record. We will discuss all of the different ways to deal with this as you are designing and moving forward with your narration.

Characters: If the characters are fictional one thing that is very important is understanding every aspect of them. For example you need to know the way they dress, walk, pause, express themselves and think. As a narrator you must put yourself in their mind and take on all of these aspects to deliver an effective narration.

If the character is fictional and you are not sure how they should talk and express themselves look to the historical record and the media to see if there are any other references to this sort of creature out there. Many times a simple Google search can take you to a historic piece of film or a piece of literature that you never knew about.

Takeaways

- Do your research.
- Practice the roles.
- Make cheat sheets so you can remember all of the details of a character.
- Relax and do not hesitate to take breaks if you lose your focus.

Fiction audiobooks, just like onions have many layers. And one of those key layers are subplots. A plot is the main story which is being told and yet the subplots are all about the other minor things which are going on in the lives of the characters at the same time. These levels of added subplots add to the interest of the listener and also add to the tension of the plot. However, it is very important if you are narrating a fiction book that you do not just focus on the main plot but understand the overarching themes of the subplots in your own work. Here are a few tips for doing just that.

Subplots:

- Make a diagram of all of the subplots in the script.

- Draw the connections like in a flow chart sort of manner from character to character.

- In some books the subplots are so complicated that they almost overwhelm the main plot. If they are very intricate and involved make certain that you are making notes and keeping track of all of the elements that will build great tension.

- Subplots are mini lessons for the characters in the course of the script. Sometimes these are also used as devices to hint at future books or spin off series which might be coming down the pike in the future.

- These are also a vested part on the part of the author to build the personality and presence of any character and make them more whole to the listener.

What is the single most important element of great writing? It is conflict. Conflict gives the reader an idea into the personalities, the history, drama and the intensity of each of these characters as well as the struggle they have with their environment. As a narrator there is nothing that is more important than using this element to continue with the action of the plot line. You want to build tension and to help move it along for the successful delivery of the work.

Conflict:

- You must use emphasis on keywords to express the passion of the characters. This passion can be excitement, hate, disgust or revenge. And yet the most important thing is to express the conflict.
- Practice saying the words with extra emphasis in the guise of the character before recording. Attempt this multiple times to make sure you are giving the most inflamed performance possible.

- Remember you must bring the conflict to life to your listeners, they have to be able to feel the conflict through your voice. This is very important because it sets the tone and mood of the story.

There you have the elements of an excellent fiction narration which will set the audience ablaze and leave them thirsting for more.

Successful Narration of a Non Fiction Book

So the first thing to consider here is that there are two kinds of nonfiction books biographical and also books on a subject. These two must be handled in a separate manner. We shall discuss this in detail:

Biographical books tell a story which actually did happen and for this reason in order to transport the listener there it is very important to nail all of the elements of the time period. As a narrator you must think about a few elements as you are designing the characters you are going to portray. Just because the book is not fiction does not mean that there should be any less attention paid to dialect, swagger, and mannerisms.

Actually it is the opposite as you are trying to embody the characters that once lived and who may be still living. Since these are actual real people, trying to portray them as they were or are is all the more important to the validity and accuracy of the story.

Biographical Narration:

- Do your research, find out where the people were born, the kinds of lives they had and flesh out these details in the portrayal.

- Consider other elements like background, age, and personal ticks of characters such as talking with a scratchy throat or anything that is historically accurate and relevant to the story.

- Look at the script and examine it for colloquialisms or other items which were popular to the time period. Practice those extensively for an accurate delivery.

Now if you are going to narrate a book on losing weight or swapping to a Paleo Diet the tone you are going to take during the narration will be a bit different. You want to ensure that your voice is pleasant, clear and informational. Think about a newscaster reading the news or a professor giving an address in front of a class. You want to ensure that your delivery as well as cadence is professional, informative and helpful to the audience.

Nonfiction Subject Audiobooks

- Speak clearly and slowly.
- Relax and do not break off into a torrent with the facts.

- Remember that part of what you are trying to do is to stimulate the interest of the reader to go further beyond the book.
- In nonfiction books on a topic, it is very important that correct attention is paid to sentences and logical stopping points. You want to keep the reader entertained and informed.
- Do not read the script like the monotone professor from Ferris Bueller and also do not pitch the book like a salesman as you are trying to inform and entertain the audience not get them to buy a used car.

Hopefully you already feel better and are ready to narrate your own book, with the thought that the audience will come back wanting more now!

Additional Super Tips on How To Perform An Amazing Narration

The importance of delivering an amazing narration can not be overstated as it is the gateway to your listener's hearts and ears. It will allow your book to resonate with them or not and it should be your goal to resonate with them. Having said that, here are some additional super tips on how to perform an amazing narration.

1. **Know Where to Put the Mic:** Make certain that you do not have the microphone to close or too far away. If it is too close the narration will be muffled and the sound quality will be poor. And too far away it may sound like you are narrating from another universe. A safe distance is within 6 to 12 inches from your face, which allows plenty of distance and closeness at the same time.

2. **Record a Practice Round before Starting the Recording:** This allows you as a narrator to warm up and also allows you to isolate any sounds which might come across as distracting in the recording. Perhaps there is a fan in the background that you don't notice while you are in the moment recording but it is picked up on the demo.

3. **Listen to Your Copy with Good Headphones:** When you play something over regular speakers you are not able to hear some of the details in the background and may not notice them. Your listener however will be probably listening with headphones so it is very important that they hear quality of this nature.

4. **Have an Easy Script:** Since you wrote it and know your writing style the narration should come easily. Make sure you think about natural starts and stops as well as transitional changes. Also print a copy of your book so you do not have to constantly stare at a small computer screen.

5. **Stand and Deliver:** Don't imagine yourself as a masterpiece theatre host, plan on standing while narrating. You will feel more focused; have better posture, breathing, and a better sound.

6. **Don't add to the Script:** Remember to stick with the script that you have in your hand. Don't consider re-writing your character's thoughts and feelings from the recording booth. Although sometimes it is possible to get wrapped up in the moment and think that you have a creative idea, the place to handle that is not while recording, regardless of how inspired you are feeling.

7. **Staying Hydrated and Having Beverages on Hand:** Drinking fluids is much more important than you would imagine when you are recording for long hours at a time. It is very important to make sure that you have clear vocal cords and a relaxed throat when narrating. Having tea as well as water available in the recording area will make things much more relaxed as well. Narrating for an extended period of time can do strange things to the voice so you must fully prepare when this occurs.

8. **Block out Plosives:** I've previously discussed plosives but just in case you forgot plosives are words with the "P" sound that tend to "pop" the microphone with a sudden burst of air. It is a challenge when recording audio to keep out these plosives as they are so natural. Here is the last warning in regards to plosives, use a pop filter!

9. **Silence is Golden:** When preparing to record it is very important to record around 10-30 seconds of silence to begin with. After recording the silence listen to it and see if there is anything in the background that might be a loud noise or a machine sound which is distracting for recording purposes.

10. **Take a Deep Breath:** Make sure you are relaxed while narrating. Don't be nervous and do not rush while reading the content. In fact, before you begin recording and during breaks make sure that you take several deep breaths. This will enable you to move through the script at a normal and comfortable rate when you record.

11. **Keep Track of all Retakes:** Make certain if you are recording different takes with different beginnings and ends that you keep a clear record. This will enable you to see where and when you have possibly had an issue you were unaware of in narration or sound. By keeping track you will know which the correct copy is at the end of the day. That is always the most challenging part. In the moment you might think you will remember and yet the second that you walk away it is very hard to remember which the correct version to use is.

12. **Decreasing Extraneous Sound:** It is all around us with children playing, birds chirping outside, and other noises kicking on and off that we do not think about on an everyday basis. And yet when you are recording it is important to try and cut these out as much as possible behind you. Is it possible that there is a padded wall? Adding a

comforter to the wall behind you is a great way to help insulate some of this sound.

Narrating to an Imaginary Audience: Things to Keep in Mind

Organization: As a narrator you must think about the logical sequence of events in every part of a book. What is the timeline and what is happening? How are you conveying these events? Are you thinking logically about all of the transition points of the text and where everything begins and ends? Remember that each sentence must be treated as an art form with all of its distinctive elements.

Compare your method to speaking in conversation with someone. You automatically think first about something that you want to say, and then you speak it. You must be mindful here as well and think about logical patterns.

Put your thoughts in logical order and then speak them to the listener. Pause constantly to consume each thought. Speak to the audience as though they are a friend and you want for them to absorb all of the information which you are passing to them moment by moment. They will feel in the moment of the text with this practice and then will find themselves wrapped in every word by utilizing this conversational technique.

Expression: You must convey every notation, accent, pause and thought when you are playing multiple roles in a manuscript. Imagine the characters and the way they are interacting with one another along with the way they speak to one another. They must be believable in every element.

The key to being a fantastic narrator is being able to convey everything including the conflict which the characters feel with one another. The listener should feel the cold of a crisp morning as well as the passion of love between two characters. Without all of these elements the delivery of the manuscript will fall flat and many elements of wonder which could have been a part of the performance will be missed.

Pace: The clip and way you narrate your book is critical. You must keep up with the rhythm and flow of the dialogue and look out for action words in the manuscript. Any time there is a verb that conveys a lot of action there are excellent ways to work around that by picking up the pace to the clip of the verb. If the main character is running, there should be some panting involved in the narration for example.

Hopefully some of these common sense super tips will give you a better idea of how to perform and deliver an amazing narration of your book. Sometimes as an author it is very easy to get lost in the black and white of the pages and not understand the intricacies of recording and narration. Learning how to do an amazing and effective recording is an excellent tool in the toolkit of any writer.

Chapter VI: How To Choose a Narrator For Your Book

Ok, so we have covered the essentials when it comes to narrating your own audiobook, but what if you don't want to travel that path? What if your preference is to have someone else narrate your book? Narrating your own book can be a big pain in the butt and I recommend that you not do it if you're not going to be fully committed or you simply lack the voice over talent to render a quality audiobook.

When you examine the audiobook marketplace you will quickly discover that there are a great deal of audiobooks that are recorded by professional narrators rather than the actual author. As an author why would you choose to hire a professional narrator? There are many solid reasons why you would do so. Let's go over a few of them.

1) **Lack of training** – Narrating a book especially a fiction book that consists of many colorful characters requires that you are skilled or trained in voice acting. If you lack this essential skill and training how would you be able to narrate a book that contains multiple characters with different personalities? Different accents?

   How would you be able to evoke and convey the different emotions and moods that are contained in the book and transport it to your listening audience? Despite the fact that we all could probably read a book out loud, this does not make us a professional narrator. A professional narrator is a person who knows how to interpret a story and record an engaging narration that is both clear and professional sounding. In my opinion you also have to have some natural ability.

2) **Voice** – You may not have the proper voice to narrate your particular book. Maybe you naturally have a high pitched voice, but your book's main character has a deep and menacing voice. Obviously in this case you shouldn't be narrating your book and you should hire a professional narrator who can match the deep and menacing voice characteristics of your main character.

Maybe you are a female but you've written your book from the perspective and the point of view of a male where it is absolutely necessary that your book be narrated with a male voice. Then obviously you have to hire a male narrator. What if you simply do not like your own voice or you are self conscious about it? You may even think that your voice really sucks. If this is the case, it behooves you to hire a professional narrator.

3) **You are not a good story teller vocally**- You may have written a hell of a story in print but that doesn't necessarily mean that you can be a good story teller of that same exact book vocally, as they each require a different set of skills.

For example, when someone is reading your writing they have to imagine what a character sounds like because they don't have the benefit of hearing that actual character's voice. However, when they listen to the audiobook they no longer have to use their imagination because they hear what a character actually sounds like through the voice of the narrator.

The narrator must be able to accurately portray and convey vocally what the author has expressed in their written work. For example, if the author wrote the following line: "He said to me in his thick French accent I love you mon cherie see you real soon". The narrator in his vocal delivery must actually speak with a thick French accent to paint a vivid picture and transport that experience to the listener.

4) **You are not an audiobook producer** – To produce an audiobook requires certain skill sets. You have to know how to properly record vocals, edit, mix and master as well as know how to

export the final product into the appropriate formats so that it can be distributed to the masses.

Most professional narrators have the ability to both narrate and produce an audiobook. So if you have yet to develop the skills necessary to produce an audiobook you can choose a professional narrator who does.

Finding and Selecting a Narrator

So where do you find a narrator for your book? The best way to find a narrator for your book is online. You can create a job posting on the various freelancer sites like freelancer.com, odesk.com or elance.com and you are certain to get many replies. Another great way that you can find narrators is through ACX.com which is pretty much the ideal conduit that connects authors with narrators.

The way the process works with ACX is the following. First of all you must be a resident of the United States and your book has to be already available on Amazon. In addition, you must be the "Rights Holder" of the book. You would register as a member of ACX. Once you are a registered member you are allowed to "claim" your book by locating it on the ACX search engine which basically consists of all the books that are presently on Amazon.

Once you have located your title you would simply select it and confirm that you have the audio rights for your book. For the purposes of ACX, once you have done this you are considered to be a "Rights Holder". The next step after claiming your book is creating a title profile for it. When you create a title profile for your book you must describe it and indicate the type of narrator that is best suited to narrate your book.

In addition, you also have to post a one or two page excerpt from your book which serves as the audition script for potential narrators. Potential narrators will automatically have access to your book once it is listed on ACX and will proactively audition to record your book.

Another way that you can find potential narrators is through ACX's database which allows you to search for narrators by genre, gender, language, accent, age, style, payments and location. Once you've selected your search criteria and perform a search, the results will render a list of narrators that meet your particular specifications. You will also be able to hear audio samples from these particular narrators.

We will get into the details that are involved in selecting a narrator specifically through ACX in a moment, but first I want to review some of the things that you should consider when choosing a narrator.

Things to Consider When Choosing a Narrator

1) **Make sure that your narrator has a voice that people can listen to.** First of all you want to make sure that your narrator has a voice that people can listen to for a long period of time. You don't want to select a narrator that will either bore your listeners to death or annoy them. Also make sure that your narrator has the appropriate voice to fit your book especially if your book contains multiple characters. This segues perfectly to number two.

2) **Make sure the audition script that you are supplying contains multiple characters.** This will allow you to hear whether or not the narrator has the ability to create distinguishing voices for each character that is involved in your story. It will also allow you to determine whether or not a narrator can flawlessly transition between characters.

3) **Look for the proper emotion, tone and cadence of voice.** The right display of emotion will instantly connect your listeners to the story. When you listen to your narrator's audition sample make sure that they are displaying the right emotion that will

connect your listeners to your story because if they are unable to connect emotionally you will definitely lose a chunk of your listeners.

It is imperative that you pay attention to the tone of the voice and the cadence of the voice which is basically the pace and rhythm of the spoken language.

4) **Pronunciation.** Make sure your narrator can pronounce words correctly. A mispronounce word can instantly distract and turn off listeners.

5) **Quality production.** Make sure that your narrator can produce a quality audiobook. Unless you plan on using someone else to mix and master your final product your narrator must know how to properly record, edit, mix and master your audiobook and be able to deliver it to you in the appropriate format which usually consist of multiple mp3 files.

6) **Solid agreement.** Make sure you have a signed agreement in place that clearly spells out the terms of the services that the narrator will be providing, the amount of compensation to be paid and the expected date of completion.

Ok now that you know the things that you should consider when choosing a narrator let's go back to our ACX discussion. Once you have listened to and reviewed your audition samples from narrators and you have found a narrator that you like, it is time for you to make an offer. There are essentially two ways that you can make an offer to a narrator for the production of your audiobook. You must decide which option is best for you before you make your offer.

The two ways are:

1) Pay for Production Deal

2) Royalty Share Deal

A **pay for production deal** is a binding agreement where you agree to pay the narrator a flat fee per finished hour of your book. A **royalty share deal** is a binding agreement where you agree to a 50-50 split with the narrator for the production of the audiobook. This is a great option if you don't have any money to pay your narrator up front.

The way that it works is when you make a sale through the ACX distribution channel which includes Audible.com, Amazon.com and the ITunes store, you and your narrator will receive a 50/50 equal split of the royalties paid out for each share. Now that exact amount of that 50/50 split depends on the price of your audiobook (which is decided individually by each ACX distribution channel) and the distribution agreement you chose with ACX.

If you choose the exclusive distribution agreement which entails a 50% royalty base you would earn 50% of the retail price of your audiobook which will then be split with your narrator under the royalty share agreement. For example, if your audiobook was priced at $20 your 50% share of that would be $10 which will then be split 50/50 with your narrator. Under this scenario you will receive $5 and your narrator will also will receive $5.

If you choose the non-exclusive distribution agreement which entails a 25% royalty base you will earn 25% of the retail price of your audiobook which will then be split with your narrator under the royalty share agreement. Using the same example of an audiobook priced at $20 your 25% share of that would equal $5 which will then split 50/50 with your narrator. Under this scenario you will receive $2.50 and your narrator will also receive $2.50.

In concluding this topic on narration if you want to have a great audiobook you must make certain that you plan out its execution as thoroughly as if you were rewriting the book one more time. Remember that this time the audience is going to have the story told to them through the art of sound. The story should be diagrammed out; the characters must be developed and practiced. The tension and reverberation of emotion should be felt in every moment of the audiobook.

Whether or not you or someone else is narrating the audiobook the end result should be the same. The brand you as an author are delivering to readers must be magical, captivating, honest and consistent every time. By doing this you will build an eager following who will await every book that you are putting out as an author.

They will hang on every word and on every moment hungering for more details about the characters. The listener will lose themselves in the intricacies of the subplots and will look eagerly at their calendars wondering when they will be able to get their next moment of being transfixed in your work.

Plan diligently as an author and do not compromise on quality for niceness. At the end of the day this is directly related to your profits, your vision, and your legacy. Happy narrating out there authors and artists alike.

Chapter VII: How To Record Your Audiobook Using Audacity

Audacity is a great free recording, mixing and editing software that doesn't require you to be a rocket scientist to use it. It is the perfect solution for producing a quality audiobook that you can be proud of. I am going to show you the steps that you have to take in order to record your audiobook and produce a final product, but first I am going to familiarize you with some of the jargon that you will need to know to begin recording in Audacity and I will also be highlighting the various features as well.

Audacity is compatible with the Mac, Windows, GNU/Linux operating systems as well as others. The first thing that you need to do in order to get started is download the software and here is that link again: http://www.audacity.sourceforge.net. After you have downloaded the software, install it and then open it up and let's review some of the items that are in the interface or control panel.

Transport toolbar - The transport toolbar is the easiest way to control playback and recording. The pause button is the first button that you see, the color of it is light blue and it enables you to pause your recording during playback. The next button is the play button and the color of it is green. This button is self explanatory as it allows you to playback the audio. The stop button follows the play button and the color of it is brown and you would use it of course to stop the recording or the playback.

The next button after the stop button is the "skip to start" button which is pink and when you click this button it will take you back to the starting point or the beginning of the audio. The next button after the "skip to start" button is the "skip to end" button which is also pink and when you click on it, it will take you to the end of the audio.

Tools toolbar – The tools toolbar contains various tools for selection of audio, volume adjustment, zooming and time shifting of audio.

Selection toolbar – The selection toolbar controls the sample rate of the project as well as adjusts cursor and region position by keyboard input. In regards to the sample rate, it is basically the number of samples of audio carried per second. 44100 Hz is the industry sample and you should choose it when recording your audiobook. ACX sample rate requirements are 44100 Hz.

Mixer toolbar – The mixer toolbar controls the output and input levels of audio devices like the microphone etc.

Meter toolbar – The meter toolbar basically displays the playback and recording levels.

Edit toolbar – The edit toolbar allows you to copy, paste, cut and trim audio. It also allows you to undo or redo your recording or edits.

Device toolbar – You would use this toolbar to select the audio host, input and output device as well as the number of input channels.

Ok let's now look at **audio tracks**. What exactly is an audio track in Audacity? An audio track is the place where your vocals or instrument is stored once it is recorded or imported from an audio source. You can use multiple audio tracks when recording in Audacity. An audio track can be stereo or mono. When you record your voice or an instrument there is a visual representation of that recording in the form of a wave that displays itself inside of a track.

You can manage and manipulate your tracks by using the track control panel that appears directly to the left side of every track. The track control panel consists of the following:

Mute button – The mute button silences the track.

Solo button – The solo button isolates and only plays that particular track.

The top slider – The top slider which is located below the mute and solo buttons is the gain control and it affects the relative volume of the track.

The bottom slider – The bottom slider which is located right below the top slider is the pan control which affects the balance between the left and right speakers.

Bit rate - The track control panel also indicates the bit rate which determines the quality of the audio data and the amount of space it takes up. 32-bit float is basically the highest quality that Audacity supports, and it is recommended that you use it when recording your audiobook.

Sample rate – The sample rate is also indicated in the track control panel.

The timeline - The timeline displays a horizontal ruler above the tracks measuring time from zero and beyond.

Now that you are familiar with some of the features in Audacity you can began recording:

Step 1 – Make sure that your USB condenser microphone is plugged in and your headphones are also plugged in so that you can monitor what you hear during recording and playback.

Step 2 – If you haven't already done so launch the Audacity program. You can do this by double clicking the Audacity icon on your desktop.

Step 3 – In this particular step you would test your microphone by speaking into it then you would appropriately adjust the levels until you get the ideal recording levels. Make sure you monitor the meter toolbar and you don't exceed 0db when you are recording because it will result in clipping which is basically a distortion of the sound.

Step 4 – You would click on the record button and begin recording the chapter of your audiobook. When you are finished recording you would simply click the stop button.

Step 5 – You would preview your audio by pressing skip to start which will return the play head to the beginning. Click play and listen to your audio.

Step 6 – After listening to the playback you would then save your unedited audio as a new Audacity project file.

Chapter VIII: Editing Your Audiobook In Audacity

After you record your chapters of your audiobook the next step is editing. When you playback your unedited track listen intently for possible errors that you made while narrating your audiobook. Look for flubbed lines, mispronounced words, long pauses, plosives, popping, clicks and undesirable mouth sounds within words that made their way onto your recording etc.

In some cases you might have to completely record over mistakes and in other cases you will simple be able to edit them out. In the editing process you will be utilizing the cut, copy, and paste tools in Audacity. You will be using the selection tool which looks like the capital letter I to select the part of the audio that you wish to cut, copy or paste to which is similar to what you would do in a Word document. To activate the selection tool all you have to do is click on it in the tool bar.

In Audacity you are able to silence unwanted noises. I use the silencing feature if I have unwanted noises that have occurred between vocal lines. However, when you use it this way you have to keep in mind that a sudden drop in background ambience can produce an awful effect. To minimize this you would fade the area around the silenced part by fading in quickly and fading out slowly.

You can also use the envelope tool to lower the volume in that particular area. To silence an area all you would have to do is highlight it and select "generate" on the toolbar menu then select silence and the silence generator is going to pop up, select "OK" and that part of the track will be silenced.

Audacity allows you to easily manipulate and move audio around by using such tools as the split function and the time shift tool. In addition, you are able to duplicate tracks to experiment with the various effects before making a final choice. One of the greatest things that Audacity allows you to do is remove noise from your recording. By utilizing the noise removal tool you can reduce constant background sounds such as hum, whistle, whine or buzz, and moderate amounts of "hiss" in your recording.

How To Remove Noise From Your Recording

To remove the noise from your recording just highlight and select a small snippet of it using the selection tool. Noise is basically anything other than your actual vocals. Just look at the waveform of the track when looking for noise. Once you have selected the snippet of noise the next step is to get a profile of it.

To get a profile of the noise you click "Effect" in the toolbar menu then you would select noise removal. The noise removal prompt appears and you would set your parameters for noise removal. The parameters that you set consist of the following:

Noise Reduction (dB) – The Noise Reduction (dB) controls the amount of volume reduction to be applied to the noise. You would set this to the lowest value that reduces the noise to an acceptable level.

Sensitivity (dB) - The Sensitivity (dB) controls how much of the audio will be considered as noise, by applying a gain to the noise thresholds.

Frequency Smoothing (Hz) - With frequency smoothing the larger the value the more the effect considers different frequencies as the same. If your noise consists of a hum or a high-pitched whistle, then you would keep this value small. However, if your noise is a hiss, then you would apply a larger value.

Attack/decay time (secs) - The Attack/decay time determines how quickly noise removal reacts. You would use a larger value if the background noise is pretty constant or if it varies rapidly you would use a smaller value.

Noise - Under the "Noise" parameter you have the remove radial button and the isolate radial button. You would select the remove button to remove the noise and before doing so you can preview the noise that you will be removing by clicking on the preview button. The isolate radial button allows you to isolate the noise and you can also preview this as well.

Once you have set your parameters for noise removal you would then click on the "get noise profile" button. Then you would go back to the toolbar menu and click on "Effect" again then select noise removal also again. You are greeted by the noise removal prompt click "OK" and the noise on your vocal track will be removed.

This information on editing may seem to be a lot, but editing in Audacity is fairly simple and easy to learn because they have tutorials readily available that you can access by clicking on the help section in the software. If you prefer to see a video demonstration on the editing capabilities of Audacity just visit YouTube.

Chapter IX: Mastering Your Audiobook In Audacity

Now that you have edited your audiobook to meet your satisfaction it is now time to master it. So what exactly is mastering? Mastering is the process of taking your recorded material and bringing out the best in it. It is simply sonic maximization. Normally if you were making a recording that not only consisted of vocals, but a variety of instruments both live and midi the process would be much more complicated, because you would be dealing with more elements and those elements would have to blend in with each other sonically.

However, since you are only dealing with vocal tracks or in some instances a vocal track with some background music the process is much easier. The main effects that you will be using in Audacity to sweeten the sound is the compressor, equalization, and normalization. Let's discuss these.

Equalization – Before compressing your vocals you want to first equalize them. Equalization is basically a way of manipulating sounds by frequency. In essence, equalization allows you to increase the volume of some frequencies while reducing the volume of others. For example, maybe you have a high pitched voice and you want to shape it by adding a little more bass frequency or "lows" to it, you can accomplish this by using the equalization tool in Audacity.

There are two ways that you can control the equalizer settings in Audacity. The first way is by drawing a curve. The second way is by adjusting the frequency sliders. Drawing curves enables you to make more precise adjustments to the equalization of your vocals while using the frequency sliders enables you to make broader changes.

These are the steps you must take in order to draw a curve in Audacity:

Step 1 – Click on "effects" in the toolbar menu and select equalization which instantly brings up the equalization tool.

Step 2 – Click on the "draw curves" radio button on the equalizer.

Step 3 – Then click in the frequency spectrum which looks like a graph to add an equalization point.

Step 4 – Once you have done this you can drag it up or down to adjust and change the settings.

If you wanted to instead adjust the frequency levels via the sliders, all you would have to do is select the "Graphic EQ" radio button then drag the frequency slider up or down to boost or reduce that frequency. To make your vocals sound clearer, I suggest that you decrease the frequencies in the graphic equalizer below 60 HZ. This takes away the low frequency rumble.

The way you equalize your vocals depends on your voice and the sound that you are trying to achieve, but essentially it will involve the manipulation of the low, middle and high frequencies.

Compression – When you are recording your vocals some parts of the recording are louder than other parts and by adding compression you make the louder parts softer so that you can balance the levels of your vocals to make them more consistent. The compressor effect reduces the dynamic range of the audio.

In Audacity and in most compressors there are essentially five levels of controls and they are:

1. **Threshold** - The threshold sets the level where compression starts to take effect. This is very easy to understand and the concept is simply this: the sounds that pass below the threshold are unchanged while the sounds that pass above the threshold become compressed.

2. **The Noise Floor** - You already know what noise is but what about the noise floor? The noise floor involves the amount of ambient noise in the environment. For example wind, rain, birds chirping etc. and the residual noise that is present in your sound system like for instance the noise that your computer fan makes or hiss.

The noise floor is the level or amplitude that represents the amount of near continuous background noise present in the signal. The noise floor in the compressor adjusts the gain on audio below this background level so as to prevent it being unduly amplified in processing.

3. **Ratio** – The ratio level in the compressor determines the amount of compression applied to the audio once it passes the threshold level. The higher you set the ratio level at the more the loud parts of the audio will be compressed. For audiobook production I recommend using a 3:1 ratio.

4. **Attack Time** - The attack time determines how quickly the compressor reacts to signals above the threshold. Generally speaking, you want your attack time to be fast.

5. **Decay Time** – Setting the decay time allows you to determine how soon the compressor starts to release the volume level back to normal after the level drops below the threshold.

Before you begin compressing your recording I suggest that you make two copies of it. One with the original sound uncompressed and one that you can work on the compression with, because if you don't like what the results are you can always go back to the original uncompressed recording.

Normalization – When you normalize a track basically what you are doing is increasing the level of the audio to maximize its volume. The way that it is normally done is the track is normalized to the highest peak level within the recording. To access the normalization feature in Audacity just select "effect" in the toolbar menu then select normalization.

After you have recorded, edited mixed and mastered your recording and you like what you hear, it is now time to save it in a format other than the Audacity file format as this will enable you to upload your audiobook to the audiobook distributors, to your website or produce an audiobook CD or MP3. It is best to first archive your recording in a Wave or AIFF format, then export it and save it as a MP3 format at 192 Kbps.

Exporting and Saving Your Audiobook To The MP3 Format

To export and save your audiobook in an MP3 format at 192 Kbps just simply go to "file" in the toolbar menu and select "export", this will bring up the dialog box where you would select the "options" button where you specify the MP3 settings. Select "constant" for your bit rate mode settings then under "quality" you would choose 192 Kbps.

You would then select the appropriate channel mode click the "OK" button then click the save button. Make sure where it says "Save as Type" MP3 files is selected. Locate the folder you are saving your recording to then click save and your audiobook will be converted to the MP3 format at 192 Kbps.

Chapter X: Creating An Audiobook Cover That Sells

People will always judge an audiobook by its cover, so you must make sure that you have a stellar cover before you begin selling and distributing your audiobook. If you already have your Kindle, paperback, or hardcover book on the market, then obviously you already have your book cover design and it is just a matter of converting it to an audiobook cover that meets the specific requirements of the major audiobook distributors such as Audible, ITunes and Amazon.

Remember that if you are a resident of the United States the quickest way to get your audiobook distributed through these sites is through ACX. ACX cover image requirements are as follows:

- The cover image must contain both the name of the title and the author.

- The cover image must be no smaller than 2400 X 2400 pixels in size.

- The resolution of the cover image can be no smaller than 72 dpi.

- The cover image must be squared and the squared cover must be a true squared cover and can't be rectangular with colored borders on the side like for example as it would be with a CD case cover or jacket.

- The cover image should be at least 24 bit.

- JPEG in RGB is the only acceptable format.

If you haven't as of yet created an audiobook cover here are some useful tips that you should consider when doing so:

1. **Check out the best audiobook covers in your book's genre.** Pay attention to the type of images that are used and the way the title is laid out and the font size not to necessarily copy them, but to get an idea of how a cover should be done.

2. **Create a book cover that is beautiful, inspirational and meaningful.** Your audiobook cover is super important and is one of the key factors in determining the success of your audiobook so make sure that it stands out and is inspiring, because if it is you have a great chance of making sales just based on the cover alone.

The opposite is also true, if your cover doesn't stand out and it is not inspiring this will affect your audiobook sales in the worst way.

3. **Make your title large enough so that it is easy to read.** Although the audiobook cover image is larger in size than the Kindle book image that is used on Amazon, the title still must be large enough so that people can read it when it is displayed on Audible, ITunes, Amazon, other audiobook retailers or your own website.

4. **Use a font that is easy to read.** Some fonts become unreadable once reduced in size so you want to make sure that you choose the appropriate font that will be easy to read and stand out.

5. **Use a quality stock image.** Whatever you do don't get an image from Google and use it, because it's 100% certain that you will be infringing on someone else's copyright. Instead use a quality stock image from Istock located at www.istock.com or Fotolia located at www.fotolia.com. The images from these sites will be of a much better quality and their terms of use will allow you to legally use the

image that you chose for your audiobook cover.

If you decide to do your own audiobook cover which I'm not personally a fan of there are two free software you can use to get the job done. One of them is a software called Gimp and the second one is Microsoft Paint. Gimp is the better of the two and has just as many features as Photoshop.

Not a fan of do it yourself covers? If that's the case, then you can simply outsource the task to a professional cover designer. Years ago this would have been an expensive proposition, but with sites like elance.com, odesk.com, freelancer.com and fiverr.com where you can actually get a splendid cover designed for just $5 that is no longer the case.

Chapter XI: How To Sell, Distribute, and Profit From Your Audiobook

Your audiobook is completed and your book cover is finished now it's time to make money. Audiobook profits are the name of the game and not coincidently the name of this book so let's dive into it by first discussing ACX.

In order for your audiobook to be eligible for upload to ACX you must be a registered member, a resident of the United States, have a U.S. mailing address, a valid U.S. Taxpayer Identification number (TIN) and you have to submit a W-9 form. In addition, you must be the rights holder of your audiobook to upload it and sell it through the ACX distribution channel.

Uploading your audiobook to ACX is fairly simply. The first thing you have to do is claim your book. You claim your book by typing the name of it in ACX's search engine and it will pull up your book from Amazon. In order for you to distribute your audiobook through ACX your book has to be in the Amazon Marketplace.

Once you have located your book on ACX's search engine you will see the following caption under your book's title: "This is my book, add it to ACX to make an audiobook". You will see a button directly under that which says "This is my book". Click on that button and another prompt will come up with the following options to choose from:

1) **I'm looking for someone to narrate and produce my audiobook**. You would only select this option if your audiobook is not yet done and you are looking for someone to narrate and produce your book.

2) **I will narrate my own book and upload the audio later**. This is self-explanatory.

3) **I have this book in audio and I want to sell it**. Since at this point you have a finished audiobook you would choose this option.

Once this option is chosen you are led to another page where you are required to first indicate what territory rights you own. If you own all of your territory rights you would select "World". Then you are asked to choose what type of distribution deal you want. There are two types of distribution agreements. Exclusive distribution and non-exclusive distribution and the one that you choose will determine how much you will earn from each audiobook sold. So it is imperative that you know the difference between the two.

Exclusive Distribution Agreement – With the exclusive distribution agreement you can only sell your audiobook through the ACX distribution channels which again includes Audible.com, Amazon.com and ITunes. You are not allowed to sell your audiobook anywhere else and that includes your own website. If you select the exclusive distribution agreement your royalty pay-out will be 50% of the listed retail price of your audiobook which ACX sets.

Non-Exclusive Distribution Agreement – With the non-exclusive distribution agreement you are allowed to sell your audiobook through the ACX distribution channels as well as through other audiobook retailers and your own website, but your royalty pay-out will be 25% of each unit sold through the ACX distribution channels.

Obviously, the type of agreement you enter into will have an impact on how much you will earn. So before rushing to make a decision you should thoroughly consider your options as well as your strategy. It is also important to note that regardless of the agreement that you choose you are entering in a legal binding agreement that gives ACX the right to distribute your audiobook for seven years. When you review both agreements you will see that they are written in plain English and are very easy to understand, but if you have trouble comprehending them you should call ACX directly or consult with an attorney.

Before I go any further since I've mentioned that the distribution agreement that you enter into should be based on your overall strategy, let's discuss a few potential options. For instance your strategy might entail scaling your audiobook by turning it into an audiobook CD, audiobook CD set or an MP3 download and selling all three versions in the Amazon Marketplace, through other audiobook retailers and on your own website in addition to having it distributed through ACX. In this particular case you would have to choose the non-exclusive distribution agreement.

However, if you could care less about selling your audiobook through other audiobook retailers and your own website then the exclusive agreement would be best for you. Personally, I usually choose the exclusive distribution agreement for pretty much all of my audiobooks because I'd rather receive 50% of each unit sold than 25%. Plus, I don't mine making my audiobook exclusively available to Audible, Amazon and ITunes because they are the leading audiobook retailers in the world who reach the vast majority of audiobook buyers.

Once you have chosen your distribution agreement on that same page that I referred to earlier you would then select the language that your book is in and of course that would be English. Then you would click on the "continue" button which will lead you to another page where you would "agree" to the audiobook license and distribution agreement after reading its contents.

When you check the agreement box and click continue you are led to a new page where you have to give a description of your book. ACX automatically pulls the description of your book from Amazon and inserts it into the description field. You are then allowed to edit it if you want. Once you are satisfied with the description of your audiobook, you must fill out the copyright information that is associated with your print book and audiobook.

This includes the following:

1. Print copyright owner's name.
2. Print copyright year.
3. Audiobook copyright owner.

You then have to select a category for your book and indicate whether it's fiction or non-fiction and also who the narrator is and the audiobook publisher. Once you have done this you are pretty much done and after you click the "submit" button your audiobook will be listed in the "projects" section where you would then click on the title of your audiobook and upload the files in an MP3 format. The MP3 format must be at 192 Kbps or it will get rejected.

In addition, to your book's files, you must also upload an opening credits audio file, a closing credits audio file and a retail audio sample which should be 5 minutes or less in length. Once you have finished uploading all of your files you will have to upload your audiobook cover. In order for your audiobook cover to be accepted it must be at least 2400 X 2400 pixels or larger.

After your audiobook cover is uploaded double check to make sure that you have uploaded all of your audio files. When you have confirmed this, click on the "I'm done" button and congratulate yourself, because after your audiobook goes through the quality control process which takes around two to three weeks your audiobook will head to retail and be available on Audible, Amazon and ITunes.

Audiobook Pricing

Unfortunately you don't get to set your own pricing for your audiobook when it is distributed through the ACX distribution channels. Audible, Amazon and ITunes independently price your audiobook and determine such price at their sole discretion. Audible determines the price of your audiobook according to the length of the recording and the following represents a general guideline on how they do it.

Under 3 hours: under $10

3 – 5 hours: $10 - $20

5–10 hours: $15 - $25

10–20 hours: $20 - $30

Over 20 hours: $25 - $35

Audiobook Royalties

ACX uses an escalator royalty system which allows you to earn up to a 90% royalty rate depending on the options you choose and based on the total amount of sales of your audiobook. For example, as mentioned previously if you choose the exclusive distribution agreement your royalty rate starts of at 50% of the retail price and then escalates 1% each time you reach a certain sales threshold.

If you narrated your own audiobook, or outsourced the task via a pay per production deal with a narrator through the ACX system which involves paying a flat fee for narration services, for every 500 sales that your audiobook makes your royalty rate increases by 1%. By the way this would also apply if you outsourced the narration of your audiobook outside of the ACX system. Here's a brief example of the escalating royalty rate under the exclusive distribution agreement.

From 0 to 500 Units-50.0%

From 501 to 1000 Units -51.0%

From 1001 to 1500 Units-52.0%

From 1501 to 2000 Units-53.0%

From 2001 to 2500 Units-54.0%

Obviously your royalty rate is increasing by 1% for every 500 sales that you make, but it reaches the max at a 90% royalty rate which in order to reach you would have to sell 20,010 units. Now if you entered in a royalty share agreement where someone narrates your book for a 50/50 split of the royalties and you selected the exclusive distribution agreement, the numbers are basically the same except you will be receiving less than you would have if you were narrating your book yourself or you just paid someone a flat fee to do it. For example, if you sold 500 audiobooks you are at the 50% royalty rate however, 25% of this would have to be shared with the narrator of your audiobook.

The way that the escalator royalty system would work under the non-exclusive distribution agreement is your royalty rate will start off at 25% and escalate 1% for every 500 audiobooks sold however, the maximum that it will reach is 70%. Here's a brief example of the escalating royalty rate under the non-exclusive distribution agreement.

From 0 to 500 Units-25.0%

From 501 to 1000 Units -26.0%

From 1001 to 1500 Units-27.0%

From 1501 to 2000 Units-28.0%

From 2001 to 2500 Units-29.0%

You will receive your royalty payments every month from Audible for the sales that you make on Audible as well as the sales that you make on Amazon and ITunes. To receive a royalty check you have to have audiobook sales of at least $50.

In addition, to receiving a check from the sales of your audiobook there are also other ways to increase your earnings through ACX. ACX offers a $25 bounty payment every time your book is one of the first three downloads by a new Audible listener on Audible.com. So if 100 Audible members downloaded your audiobook you can expect to receive $2,500 in addition to your regular royalty payment. How cool is that?

Whispersync for Voice and Immersion Reading

Audible offers Whispersync for voice and immersion reading and this is another way that you can increase your earnings with both your audiobook and your Kindle book. Let me explain what they are. Whispersync for voice is a breakthrough technology that allows you to switch back and forth between reading a Kindle book and listening to the companion Audible audio book without losing your space. For example, say if you've listened half-way through chapter 7 of an audio book while in your car but instead of listening you have the urge to read more of the book once you got home, your Kindle will bring you in the text exactly to where you stopped listening.

Whispersync for immersion reading allows readers to synchronize Kindle text with the Audible audio version of the book. Also while they are reading, the text in the E-book is highlighted as the audio track moves along, making it easier for the reader to follow along.

Audible offers your audiobook the opportunity to be made available for sale as a companion to the Kindle book for customers who want to make use of the Whispersync and immersion reading features of the Kindle. This will result in increase sales for both your audiobook and your Kindle book because people will be looking to utilize these great features. However, to be eligible your audiobook must meet certain requirements. One of those requirements is that your audiobook must match the text of the Kindle book version of it. ACX rules also require that your audiobook has a 97% sync rate.

What if you're not a U.S. Resident?

If you live outside of the United States and you want to sell your audiobook on Audible, ITunes or Amazon you can, you just aren't able to do it through ACX. The way that you can get it distributed on Audible is by sending them an email at internationalpartner@audible.com and asking them permission to upload your audiobook. They require basic and straight forward information like what you are publishing, if you have other books to come, and if it is original work.

In order for your audiobook to be considered for distribution on Audible:

1. Your content must be unique. (not something on the public domain or PLR)

2. It must be owned by you and you are able to legally publish it.

3. It must be a good quality recording.

You can also get your audiobook on Audible and ITunes as well as other audiobook distributors by using an aggregator like Open Book Audio located at www.openbookaudio.com. Open Book Audio doesn't charge you any upfront setup or processing fees for listing your title with them. Instead, they charge a percentage of the sales of your title after the retailers have taken their cut.

Here's how it works: If your audiobook was selling for $30 and the retailer took a 50% cut ($15), your net revenue would be $15. Open Book Audio would take a 30% cut of that amount ($4.50), and you would be left with the balance which is $10.50.

To get your audiobook listed with Open Book Audio the first step would be to contact them and let them know that you're interested in submitting your audiobook for consideration. They review every audiobook submitted to them before they accept it. Some of the factors that they consider when deciding whether or not to accept an audiobook are:

Audio quality
Narrator quality
Length of audiobook
Subject matter
Overall performance

You can send your audiobook to them digitally and they will instruct you how to send it to them once you have contacted them or you can send them a CD or DVD version of your book to the following address:

Open Book Audio
ATTN: Book Submission
PO BOX 3304
Redmond, WA 98073

Selling Your Audiobook CD on Amazon

You can sell your audiobook in a CD format on Amazon. If you become a seller in the Amazon Marketplace you are allowed to sell a variety of products. However, for your purposes you are only interested in selling your audiobook in a CD format. Why would you want to make available your audiobook in a CD format? Simply because many people still listen to CDs and you want to be able to offer that segment of the marketplace that choice plus it's an additional revenue stream for you.

Of course it's quite easy to create an audiobook CD version of your book. All it takes is really sequencing the chapters of your audiobook files in order to be burned to a CD and using a print on demand fulfillment CD service. You want to choose a print on demand fulfillment service because you don't really want to go out and invest in a bunch of inventory and you don't want to have any upfront costs. You basically just want to order your audiobook CDs when you get actual customer orders or when you choose to participate in the Amazon Advantage fulfillment program where they require for you to have a certain amount of inventory in stock to fulfill your orders.

The best print on demand fulfillment CD service is a company called Kunaki located at the following website address www.kunaki.com. Kunaki is basically a print on demand digital manufacturing service that has no minimum order requirements. You can manufacture 1 CD or 10,000 CDs it really doesn't matter.

The way that the process works is you have to first design and configure your product (case, disc, inserts, cover art, contents) with their publishing software. The software will render a precise 3-D replica of your product and will let you modify and review different possibilities and options. The software then compiles your product's content, packaging, and art-work into a single digital file and uploads it to Kunaki's facility.

When you are ready to order, you would just enter your customer's information and make your payment, and Kunaki will manufacture your audiobook CD and ship to your customer a full-color, glossy, fully assembled, cellophane-wrapped, high-quality, retail-ready CD that contains a UPC bar code. By the way the UPC bar code is absolutely free.

The cost for you to order CDs at Kunaki is $1.00 per unit when you order 5 or less CDs and included in this price are:

- Manufacturing
- Assembly
- Full color CD printing

- Jewel case
- A Full color 2-panel insert
- A Full color tray card
- Cellophane wrapping
- A UPC bar code
- 24 hour manufacturing

When you order 6 or more CDs the price is $1.75 per unit and both prices that I quoted does not include the shipping costs that are involved. Now that you know how to utilize a print on demand fulfillment manufacture CD service to manufacture your audiobook CDs, let's discuss how you would sell it on Amazon.

The Amazon Marketplace and Amazon.com Advantage

There are two ways in which you can sell your audiobook CD on Amazon:

1. Through the Amazon.com Advantage Program

2. Through the Amazon Marketplace

Advantage is a self-service consignment program that enables you to sell your audiobook CD directly on Amazon.com. The way that it works is you have to first join the Advantage Program and the cost of doing so is $29.95 for a 1 year membership. Once you are registered as a member you would then add your audiobook CD title to your Advantage account.

Amazon would then order a conservative quantity of audiobook CDs from you and their goal for doing this is they want to make sure that they have enough quantity to meet current demand as well as possible future orders in the weeks ahead.

Once your audiobook CD inventory is received by Amazon it is stored in one of their fulfillment centers and it will be available for purchase on Amazon. When your audiobook CD is purchased on Amazon's site they will ship those orders out for you.

I must point out that in order to sell your audiobook CD on Amazon it must contain a scannable ISBN, UPC, or EAN bar code and be cellophane wrapped. That's why I strongly suggest that you use Kunaki as your print on demand CD service, because not only do they provide you with a free scannable UPC bar code, your audiobook CD is also cellophane wrapped and they will in addition manufacture and drop-ship your audiobook CDs to Amazon and restock them when needed.

How and When You Get Paid by The Amazon Advantage Program

If you choose to sell your audiobook CD through Amazon's Advantage program you will earn 45% of the listed price of your item and Amazon gets the remaining 55%. So if you were selling your audiobook CD for $20 you will earn $11 for each unit sold and Amazon will receive $9.

You will receive payment for your audiobook CDs sold through the Advantage program automatically at the end of the month following the month in which your product is sold. For example, for items sold in the month of February, they will pay you at the end of March. Payment can be made to you by Electronic Funds Transfer (EFT) to a U.S. bank account or by paper check. If you opt to receive payment via check, your payment will not be disbursed until you reach a threshold of $100 and there is a $15 processing fee assessed to each check.

The great thing about selling through the Amazon Marketplace and the Advantage program is that you are allowed to set the pricing of your audiobook CD giving you the ultimate control.

Amazon Marketplace

You can sell your audiobook CD through the Amazon Marketplace, but it requires a Pro Merchant Subscription to do so. The cost of a Pro Merchant subscription is $39.99 per month. Whatever you do (unless you already have a Pro Merchant subscription on Amazon because you are selling other products) don't pay the $39.99 per month fee to have your audiobook CD listed in the Amazon marketplace.

Here's what you do instead. Amazon offers a 30 day free trial for a Pro Merchant Subscription and you should use it to list your audiobook CD for free. The way that you would list your audiobook CD is via your Seller Central account. Seller Central is the Web interface used to manage all aspects of selling on Amazon.com. There you can add product information, make inventory updates, manage orders, and manage payments though a suite of Web-based and downloadable tools.

A smart way to list your inventory without never having to update the quantity again is by entering in a high number where it asks you how many units that you have in stock. The number that I normally put is 5,000 units that way I don't have to worry about it for a little while.

How and When You Get Paid As a Seller in Amazon's Marketplace

As a seller in Amazon's marketplace you are responsible for shipping out your own audiobook CDs for customers who have ordered it. The great thing about that is Amazon collects from the customer the shipping cost which you can then apply when you ship the item. That is one of the main differences between selling via the Amazon Marketplace and selling via the Advantage program.

Another huge difference is the amount of money you make from each unit sold. As a seller in the Amazon Marketplace you earn about 85% of the total list price for each unit sold. Amazon makes about a 15% commission. I don't know about you but I'd rather make 85% over the 55% that the Advantage program pays so as I result I ship out my own audiobook CDs for now.

In addition, when you sell via the Advantage program, Amazon doesn't share your customer's information with you like their name and address. On the other hand as a seller in Amazon's Marketplace those details are shared with you which allows you to build and cultivate a customer base.

You get paid from Amazon services for the sales that you have made through the Amazon Marketplace when they have "settled" your account. This occurs every 14 days. Whenever your account has been settled and you have a positive balance from your sales Amazon transfers your funds to your bank account using an Automated Clearing House (ACH) or electronic funds transfer.

Chapter XII: Promoting and Marketing Your Audiobook

Audiobook promotion and marketing is pretty much the same as marketing and promoting a digital, paperback or hardcover book. Nonetheless, let's go over some fantastic ways that you can promote and market your audiobook.

YouTube

One of the hottest ways that you can promote and market your audiobook is on YouTube. Video allows you to create and share remarkable and engaging content with your potential audience in a way that plain text will never match.

Let's face it most people love videos, because it allows them to connect visually and aurally in a fun way to the subject matter as opposed to looking at and reading an advertisement in a newspaper or a magazine. Tell me which one would you prefer?

Here are some useful tips on how you can you use videos and YouTube to market your audiobook to your targeted niche:

Create a Channel

If you plan on creating several audiobooks you should create a YouTube channel showcasing them. This allows YouTube users to subscribe to your channel, and permits you to send out emails to the ones who have subscribed to you. Link your videos to Facebook, Twitter, Google+, and any other websites that could increase exposure.

Establish Your Brand

Make sure to include the cover design of your audiobook at the beginning or end of your videos and make sure you also include a link back to your website in the description area. Establish a personality or "voice" for your videos. Make sure that it matches your branded tone which you have established through other marketing channels. Take every chance you can to let your videos stand out. Building your brand is just as important as selling your audiobook.

Keywords are important

It is important that you include your main keywords of your audiobook in your video's description, title and tag section. Keywords allow your targeted users to locate your video by typing relevant keywords into the YouTube search engine. Keywords also enable the major search engines like Google, Yahoo and Bing to include your video in their search results.

Exploring the YouTube Community

Since YouTube is a social networking site you should find ways to get viewers to your video within the YouTube community. Comment on other people's videos that have the same subject matter as your audiobook. This may inspire them to visit your channel, view your videos and also leave comments.

Embed your audiobook video on your website

YouTube allows you to embed videos on your website via HTML code. This is very useful because you can use this feature to put your YouTube hosted videos on your site so that your website's visitors can also view your videos. Embedding your YouTube videos on your site instead of personally hosting them, saves on bandwidth and results in a faster download for your website's visitors.

Press Releases

A press release is a great way to let the masses know about your audiobook. It is also an effective way to get traffic to your website as your link is included in the press release. There are tons of sites online where you can submit your press release, some paid and others free. To maximize your results, you should probably submit to as many free ones as you can and also consider investing in a paid service to distribute your press release. In my opinion the top paid press release distribution company is PRWeb and you can access them by visiting www.prweb.com.

Realizing the great opportunity that press releases offer, a lot of authors are using strategies to ensure that their press releases receive maximum exposure. If you have never written a press release before, then you need to become familiar with the standards and format expected of a press release. You may want to spend some time researching how press release writing is done before diving in, but here are some general instructions:

1) **Write a killer headline.** People usually skim through headlines searching for things that jump out at them and as such your headline is one of the most important parts of the entire press release. You need to focus on making it attractive to get people's attention. Your headline should be unique and different, and you must make it stand out from the crowd and all the clutter. Your headline should always be written in title case.

2) **Back it up with a strong sub-headline to add more details**. The sub-headline can be used to highlight other important points you wish to bring forth to the reader's attention. The ultimate objective and goal of the headline and sub headline is to reel the reader in so that they read the rest of your press release and hopefully take action.

3) **Answer the basic questions in the lead.** The next part of your press release is the lead, which typically addresses all the particular details of

your story. Here you would discuss what your audiobook is about, some of the characters, the setting of the story etc.

4) **Tell the story using the body of your press release.** This is where you want to include all the most important information related to your story. The body usually includes 2-4 short paragraphs and normally includes a quote somewhere within it from a key person involved in the news story (in this case, it is probably you!)

5) **Last comes the boilerplate, similar to a byline.** The boilerplate is the last part of your press release. It's similar to an "about us" section that is typically four to five sentences long.

6) **A final note on formatting**. At the end of your press release, you should always add the number symbol three times in a row with no spaces on a separate line. This is standard formatting for press releases and helps them to determine the end of your story. It would look like this ###, but it would be on its own line.

Of course, if you're not feeling confident enough to write your own press release, you can simply outsource the task. In fact, many press release distribution sites also offer writing services if you have the budget and aren't sure you can write one on your own.

Ezine Advertising

A clever way to promote and market your audiobook is through ezine advertising. What's an ezine? It's an electronic newsletter or magazine. Ezines are delivered to subscribers by email or they are simply made available online. The great thing about ezines are that they are highly targeted making it easier for you to find an audience that would be interested in the subject matter of your audiobook.

The best way to locate specific ezines in your audiobook's niche is by utilizing Charlie Page's Directory of Ezines located at the following web address:

http://www.directoryofezines.com

But before you embark on your promotion and marketing campaign via ezines, here are a few things you need to consider:

- **The ezine's niche** – You want to make sure that you advertise in ezines that can reach your target audience of your audiobook or your marketing won't be effective.

- **The ezine's amount of subscribers** – You want to know how many subscribers an ezine has before advertising, because you want to get the most for your money. Some of the smaller ezines (less than 15,000) have to charge more for advertising or they will go out of business. While the medium (20,000 – 80,000) and larger size ezines (80,000 and up) don't have to engage in that sort of practice and as a result they actually cost less per thousand readers.

Another advantage of advertising in medium and large size ezines is that they usually archive their issues on their website which gives you extended advertising exposure.

- **Make sure that your ad is well written** – An ezine ad that is well written can generate a huge response, while a poorly written one will obviously have the opposite effect. So make sure that your ad is well written and it stands out. The job of your ad should be to sell the click that will get them to visit your website or blog.

When they arrive at your site or blog they should be greeted with a sign up form that is linked to an autoresponder. This will allow you to capture their information and do a series of follow-ups that will hopefully lead to audiobook sales.

There are mainly 3 different ezine advertising formats that are available to you and here are those ad formats:

Classified ads – This is the least expensive and based on my personal experience it is also the least effective because the ads are grouped with so many other classified ads that are also vying for the same attention. Most ezines offer free classified advertising when you sign up as a subscriber.

Sponsor ads – Sponsorship ads are way more responsive than classified ads so they cost more. An ezine normally has 2 to 3 sponsor ads per issue and they are usually located at the top of the issue for higher visibility.

Solo ads – These are stand alone ads that an ezine sends out separately from its issue to their subscribers. Solo ads get the most exposure, so therefore they are more expensive than sponsor and classified ads. Solo ads allow you to include more details about your audiobook.

Book Trailers

Book trailers are also a great way to market and promote your audiobook. It is an effective and exciting way to build a buzz for your book. If you don't know what a book trailer is here's what it is in a nutshell. It is basically a marketing tool that uses visuals to grab the attention of viewers and get them interested enough so that they will seek out your audiobook.

You can create your own book trailer by using such free programs as Windows Movie Maker or you can outsource the task to companies that specialize in creating book trailers. Here are a few of those companies.

Circle of Seven Productions
(http://www.cosproductions.com/)

Authorlink
(http://www.authorlink.com/about/avproduction.php)

Blazing Trailers
(http://www.blazingtrailers.com/submit.php)

Living Jacket (http://livingjacket.com/)

If you decide to create your own book trailer these are some of the basic requirements:

- Images, photographs AND at least one short video or animation clip.
- At least some text on the screen for part of the trailer. (a short quote from an editorial review can work great for this.)
- You can either narrate your own book trailer or outsource the task. Regardless of your choice the bottom line is your book trailer needs narration.
- Music clip.

After you have produced your book trailer you have to market it. We have already mentioned YouTube as a possibility, but there are also book trailer submission sites that you can use to expose your book trailer. Here are a few of those sites.

BookTrailers.net (http://www.book-trailers.net)

Comic Book Trailers
(http://www.comicbooktrailers.com)

Clean Book Trailers
(http://cleanbooktrailers.blogspot.com)

If Books Could Talk
(http://bookvideos.wordpress.com)

Bookcaster (http://www.bookcaster.com)

Book Riot (http://www.bookriot.tv)

Watch the Book (http://www.watchthebook.com)

TrailerSpy (http://www.trailerspy.com)

Social Media

In this day and age I know that you are all too familiar with social media and its use as a marketing and promotion tool. The great thing about social media is that it offers a unique and fun opportunity to engage with your audience and nurture your leads without being a pushy salesperson. In fact, social media sites are an author's best friend in this regard. Here are the main ones that you should definitely use as a vehicle to communicate and engage your audience.

Twitter

Twitter of course is one of the most popular social media sites in the world and is an excellent source that you can use to promote your audiobook. You are able to send "tweets" made up of 140 characters. You gain an audience on Twitter by people "following" you.

If you're new to Twitter, here are some useful tips for how to use the site effectively: Use hashtags because they are very useful on Twitter. Hashtags are words with the number symbol tacked on to the beginning. Hashtags are a great way to organize and group your tweets based on the different types you post to your Twitter account. Use them to identify which tweets are about what.

Be sure to make good use of the right keywords when tweeting anything about or related to your audiobook. If your audiobook is a paranormal romance, for example, then include those keywords in your tweets and it will be easier for people to find them. If you use other sites like Facebook, LinkedIn and Google+, be sure to link up your Twitter account with your profiles on these particular sites so that your tweets will appear on all of your profiles for effective cross-promotion.

Facebook

Facebook as you probably know already is the top social media site in the world and can be useful for promoting your audiobook. You should set up a Facebook page for your audiobook and once you have done this you should join relevant Facebook groups. If you're a romance writer, search for groups of people who fit into this category as well. You should also network with others who are authors in your book's genre. Building new relationships with fellow authors can serve you well as they can make outstanding brand ambassadors for your audiobook.

Google+

Google+ is relatively new to the social media scene. It currently has well over 100 million members to date. Marketing on Google+ is a relatively new concept but here are some tips to help you get going. The first you should do after creating an account on Google+ is make sure that the settings are allowing you search visibility. In this section of your settings, choose the option that says "Help others find my profile in search results".

Then you should create a customized profile URL. Make sure to keep in mind branding yourself as an author when you create your customize profile URL. Next you should fill out your profile information because if you leave this blank when potential customers visit your customer page or profile they may immediately dismiss you if there is little to no information provided in your profile.

When you're filling out your profile make sure to indicate that you are an author and you have published an audiobook and include the link to the book so that your visitors have the opportunity to purchase it. Also make sure that you include people in your Google+ "circle" who are relevant to your book's cause. By that I mean you should be selective about who you add to your circles. Just like on sites such as Twitter, you should avoid falling into the follow-for-following trap. Just because someone adds you does not mean you should or need to add them in return.

LinkedIn

LinkedIn is a site for professionals and can be highly useful as a promotional tool if your audiobook is in the business genre. While LinkedIn has many of the standard features found on other social sites, like profiles and status updates, it also has a unique feature called the Reading List application by Amazon you can utilize to market your audiobook. You can add the Reading List application to your profile which lets your connections see which books you are currently reading. Use this tool to subtly promote your audiobook.

Chapter XIII: Conclusion

As much as writing a masterpiece is a labor of love, converting it into an audiobook is an amazing piece of work which requires skill, precision, and execution. It does not just involve sitting in a bean bag chair and reading your book's manuscript through a cheap head set and a bad computer. It offers all of the details and intricacy of becoming a voice over artist for the ostensible reason of sharing your story and your vision with the rest of the world.

Creating a home studio is not rocket science and can be easily accomplished with but a few pieces of equipment, and a silent working area. The most challenging part of the process in my estimation is not the part of setting up a studio, but the part of learning and understanding the different elements involved in storytelling.

The thing which sets apart storytelling and the medium of sound from all other kinds of narration and media sharing is that the author by becoming the main narrator of the story becomes the gateway not through just the pen but through the psychology of the reader. The role of the ancient narrator or bard is a very sacred one. Before the days of the written word many famous works were never written down and were merely repeated and shared with audiences from the memory of the story teller.

In the past stories like the Iliad and the Odyssey would change from version to version and bard to bard. Many of the bards were actually illiterate and had nothing to rely on to ply their crafts but their memories and their skill to tell a clear and imaginative story for the listener. As an author you take on this most sacred role of the bard by being not only the creator of the story, but being the mechanism through which the audience is able to understand and to feel the events of the story or the subject matter. Always remember and never forget that great narration brings a book to life.

The step to create your audiobook is a tremendous one in the right direction as you will see your profits; your confidence, your bank account and your repertoire grow significantly. In closing, I hope that you have learned a great deal from this book and you apply its fundamental and principles to ensure that your audiobook becomes a roaring success.

I have two other amazing books that can also help you as an author and self publisher. They are: **How To Promote Market and Sell Your Kindle Book:** Amazon Kindle Publishing and Marketing Promotion Guide and **The Fine Art of Writing the Next Best Seller on Kindle**. These two books are available in Kindle, paperback and audiobook format.

Other books that I have also authored and you might find of interest to you are the following:

How To Create A Profitable Ezine From Scratch

The Secrets Of Making $10,000 on Ebay in 30 Days

The Complete Guide To Investing in Gold And Silver: Surviving The Great Economic Depression

How To Sell Any Product Online:"Secrets of The Killer Sales Letter"

How To Make A Fortune Using The Public Domain

Search Engine Domination: The Ultimate Secrets To Increasing Your Website's Visibility And Making A Ton Of Cash

Creative Real Estate Investing Strategies And Tips

How to Make Money Online:"The Savvy Entrepreneur's Guide To Financial Freedom"

How to Overcome Your Self-Limiting Beliefs & Achieve Anything You Want

The Secrets of Finding The Perfect Ghostwriter For Your Book

The Creative Real Estate Marketing Equation: Motivated Sellers + Motivated Buyers = $

How To Start An Online Business With Less Than $200

How To Market Your Business Online and Offline

Good Luck and Much Success,

Omar Johnson